I Believe in Love Study Guide

I Believe in Love Study Guide

For *I Believe in Love*
by Fr. Jean C.J. d'Elbée

by Rita Brandt Ford

SOPHIA INSTITUTE PRESS
Manchester, New Hampshire

Printed in the United States of America

Cover design: Coronation Media in collaboration with Perceptions Design Studio.

On the cover: Image of St. Thérèse © Office Central de Lisieux; "Country road" (78600310) © Qba from Poland / Shutterstock.com.

Sophia Institute Press
Box 5284, Manchester, NH 03108
1-800-888-9344

www.SophiaInstitute.com

Library of Congress Cataloging-in-Publication Data

Ford, Rita Brandt.
I believe in love study guide : for I believe in love by Fr. Jean C.J. d'Elbée / by Rita Brandt Ford.
pages cm
ISBN 978-1-62282-250-8 (pbk. : alk. paper)
1. Christian life—Catholic authors—Miscellanea. 2. Love—Religious aspects—Catholic Church—Miscellanea. 3. Thérèse, de Lisieux, Saint, 1873-1897—Miscellanea. 4. Elbée, Jean du Coeur de Jésus d'. Croire à l'amour. I. Title.
BX2350.3.F67 2014
248.4'82—dc23

2014040332

6th printing

Contents

Before You Begin

As you start this book, consider:

1. Where do you feel you are on your spiritual journey?

2. What are you hoping to get out of this program?

Conference 1

Love for Love

Questions for meditation and discussion

1. St. Thérèse said, "In the evening of this life, I shall appear before You with empty hands." (page 7)

   What does this mean to you? How can you begin "emptying your hands"?

2. "As if that were not enough, He invented the Eucharist: a God who makes Himself into bread, a little host, in order

to descend onto our lips and into our hearts, to bridge all distance between Himself and us." (page 9)

Does reading this give you a different understanding of the Eucharist?

3. "Never let your past sins be an obstacle between you and Jesus." (page 12)

   How have your sins been an obstacle? How can we overcome this?

4. "If you have been loved like this, you must love in return, give love for love. 'I have loved you; you must love. I have given you my Heart without reserve, in order to have your

heart without reserve. I have put no limit on my love; you must put no limit on yours.'" (pages 13–14)

How are you giving love for love? Where are you putting limits on your love?

5. Father d'Elbée points out all the things Jesus did *not* ask Peter (are you wise? virtuous? capable of leading? and so forth). He asks only, "Do you love me?" (page 14)

   Because doubting who we are keeps us from fully loving God, what reasons do you give yourself for not *completely* loving God? ("I am not ________________ enough.")

6. "The Cross, taken up hesitantly, is crushing; taken smilingly, by free will, and with love, it will carry you much more than you carry it." (page 18)

   What are your crosses taken up smilingly? What are your crosses taken up hesitantly? How do they differ?

7. Do you fear what God will ask you to do? If yes, why? (page 21)

8. Do you think you are a joy for Jesus? In what ways do you bring Him joy? (page 22)

This week's challenge

Choose one "hesitantly" taken-up cross in your life and carry it smilingly. What difference did doing this make?

Conference 2

Humble Confidence

Review the challenge from conference 1: Choose one "hesitantly" taken-up cross in your life and carry it smilingly. What difference did doing this make?

Questions for meditation and discussion

1. "This word, *confidence*, summarizes the three theological virtues: faith, hope, and charity—sovereign virtues which bring all the others in their train." (page 25)

   How do faith, hope, and charity relate to confidence? Is it possible to have confidence in God's love for us without these virtues?

2. "I, too, would like to find an elevator to lift me up to Jesus, for I am too little to climb the rough stairway of perfection." (page 27)

   What is your "rough stairway"? How can we find the gentle elevator?

3. "We have been trained in the habit of looking at our dark side, our ugliness, and not at the purifying Sun." (page 29)

   Under what circumstances do you most often look at your dark side? In what way can we minister to those in our lives (children, spouses, and friends) to look to the purifying Sun?

4. "Remember that each time you pick yourself up after a fall, the feast of the prodigal son is renewed." (page 34)

   How do you approach the confessional?

5. "We do not dance enough in the spiritual life." (page 35)

   Can you think of a time when you were moved to "dance in the spiritual life"?

6. "How many young people have lost the Faith, not from having fallen, but from not having been helped, with love,

to pick themselves up again as many times as was necessary?" (page 35)

The primary goal of parents is to get their children to heaven. Are you teaching your children, your grandchildren, your nieces and nephews, or any other children in your life about God's infinite mercy so that when they fall, they will have the humble confidence to "rise up and go to my Father" (cf. Luke 15:18)?

7. Regarding the good thief: "A whole life of sin, one humble and confident look toward the Crucified, and there was the first canonized saint, and canonized by Jesus Himself! A thief who stole Heaven!" (page 36)

   Jesus is telling us that there is always hope and a way to Heaven. Is there some stumbling block in your life that you have given up on correcting?

8. "We sometimes make a prayer of the words for which He reproached His Apostles: 'Lord, save us; we are perishing!'" (page 41)

   Do you pray with confidence?

This Week's Challenge

"Your Father in Heaven clothes you again in His most beautiful cloak, puts a ring on your finger, and tells you to dance with joy. In a living faith, you will not approach the confessional with dragging feet, but as if you were going to a feast, even if you have to make a great effort each time to humble yourself and to conquer the monotony of the routine.

"After the absolution, you should dance like the prodigal son did at the request and for the joy of his father." (pages 34–35)

Approach the confessional as if you are preparing for a feast.

Conference 3

Unshakeable Confidence

Review the challenge from conference 2: Approach the confessional as if you are preparing for a feast.

Questions for meditation and discussion

1. St. John Vianney said, "God's greatest pleasure is to pardon us." (page 56)

    Have you felt God's pleasure after receiving the sacrament of Reconciliation?

2. St. John Vianney also said, "The good Lord is more eager to pardon a repentant sinner than a mother to rescue her child from the fire." (page 57)

   This statement expresses God's great urgency to forgive us. Do you feel a sense of urgency to forgive and to be forgiven?

3. "It is good to say, 'Jesus, make reparation for me; supply for me.' It is better to say, 'Jesus, I know—I am sure that You will do it.'" (page 60)

   Which version better reflects the way you pray?

4. "Therefore, never be discouraged by your faults. Begin by not being astonished at them. A little child who does not know how to walk is not astonished at stumbling and falling with each step he takes." (pages 64–65)

   Are you astonished at or discouraged by your faults?

5. "Let us love our littleness." (page 72)

   What are some ways we can make ourselves "little"?

6. "Pure love is realized in pure faith and pure faith is realized in darkness in the same way as 'strength is perfected in weakness.'" (page 78)

Can you think of a time when you experienced darkness or weakness? When the darkness lifted, did you feel stronger in your faith?

This week's challenge

"We have all had this temptation at one time or another. 'I have promised Him so much, I have made so many resolutions, and I will always fall again; it is impossible that He does not get tired of it.'

"It is a kind of blasphemy to say that, because it is to limit a mercy which has no limit. It is to doubt the patience, the indulgence, the untiring clemency of Jesus. It is not He who grows weary of us; it is we who grow weary of looking at our ugliness." (page 62)

Focus this week on *not* looking at your "ugliness," but dwell on the beauty God sees in you. Describe your experience. Notice in what ways doing this changes your behavior and perhaps the behavior of those around you.

Conference 4

Abandonment to Jesus

Review the challenge from conference 3: Focus this week on *not* looking at your "ugliness" but dwell on the beauty God sees in you. Describe your experience. Notice in what ways doing this changes your behavior and perhaps the behavior of those around you.

Questions for meditation and discussion

1. Throughout this conference, "abandonment" is defined in many ways. Find some of the ways it is defined. Which definition speaks to you the most? Why?

2. The Eucharist is discussed on page 82 ("The Eucharist transforms our souls into Jesus through love") and page 83 ("We bid Him come, but we do not permit Him to enter"). What can you actively do to get the most out of receiving the Body and Blood of Christ?

3. "If He destroys my little plans, I kiss His adorable hand. It is because He wants to realize His own, which are more beautiful anyway than those which I could have made myself." (page 89)

   Have you ever thought of God's plan for you as "beautiful"?

4. "It is said that the Devil makes the gravity of the sin appear to be less during the temptation and greater after the fall." (pages 95–96)

   Do you think knowing this will help you to avoid sin?

5. "How many causes of joy for Him are in us! What more does He see? All you have done for Him: your prayers, your good impulses, all the acts which, in the course of your life, have been determined by your faith, your hope, and your love; your acts of generosity, your acts of charity, especially which you have forgotten, because they are engraved in His Heart." (page 97)

   Can you think of some things you have done for Him that are now "engraved in His Heart"?

6. Remember in conference 3 St. John Vianney is quoted as saying, "God, at the moment of absolution, throws our sins over His shoulder. He forgets them; He annihilates them; they shall never reappear" (page 57). At the same time He is engraving on His Heart all that we have done for Him.

   Do you think this will help you to return more frequently to the sacrament of Reconciliation?

7. God refused the prayer of St. Monica for her son St. Augustine, in order to answer her greater prayer (see pages 101–102).

   Have you seen similar circumstances in your life (failures that are victories)? Has this increased your trust in God (abandonment)?

This week's challenge

Put the following passage into action:

I promise You, Jesus, to worry about nothing consciously, voluntarily, deliberately. As soon as I find myself worrying, I shall listen to Your gentle voice saying to me, "Let me do it. Am I not here with you, in you?" and I shall say unconditionally, "O Jesus, I thank You for everything," for You always expect that of me. (pages 97–98)

Conference 5

Great Desires, Humility, and Peace

Review the challenge from conference 4: Put the following passage into action:

> I promise You, Jesus, to worry about nothing consciously, voluntarily, deliberately. As soon as I find myself worrying, I shall listen to Your gentle voice saying to me, "Let me do it. Am I not here with you, in you?" and I shall say unconditionally, "O Jesus, I thank You for everything," for You always expect that of me. (pages 97–98)

Questions for meditation and discussion

1. "In order to give Jesus love for love, we must be souls of desire. Nothing great ever comes about without great desires. They are the mainspring, the driving force. If they are lacking, everything is dull and lifeless."(page 115)

   Think of a time when you had a desire so great for something that you were driven to achieve it. What do you desire now? Will attaining that goal give greater glory to God?

2. "How many souls I have met who have experienced these beautiful enthusiasms, yet, in admitting their weakness, their apparent mediocrity, their lack of progress, have let themselves little by little be overrun by discouragement." (page 118)

   Has this happened to you? Is there a desire you have about which you feel discouraged?

3. "Amen, I say to you, unless you be converted, and become as little children, you shall not enter into the kingdom of Heaven. Whoever therefore shall humble himself as this

little child, he is the greatest in the kingdom of Heaven." (page 120)

In what way can humbling yourself help you to achieve your great desires?

4. "By myself I can do nothing, but 'He who is all-powerful has done great things in me.'" (page 126)

   "This does not mean that those who have received natural gifts ought not to rejoice in them. These gifts are a part of our predestination; they are in the plan of God's love for us." (page 128)

   What natural gifts were you given to help you glorify God and achieve your great desires?

5. "A ravishing form of humility is simplicity. It is the charm of those who know how to put themselves in their proper place and are not puffed up in their own eyes." (page 130)

   Can you think of someone in your life who can be described in this way? In what way can you imitate that person?

6. "God speaks to us in two ways: He speaks in the intimacy of the mind and heart by interior lights, by touches of His grace, by good inspirations, and by holy desires, and He speaks externally by visible legitimate authority. If there is a conflict between the two, which must take precedence? Which will be the will of God? Always and everywhere the word of the external authority." (page 133)

   You can rely on the Church always to be the moral authority, even when your feelings are in conflict with the Church. Thus, you can be assured of the right path. Does this give you a feeling of peacefulness?

7. "It is a duty for you to spread this sweet and joyful peace around you … 'not like judges of peace, but like angels of peace.'" (page 139)

   How can you be an angel of peace in your home, at work, at school, toward a stranger?

This week's challenge

Put humility into action this week by honestly putting yourself in the last place in some way.

Conference 6

Fraternal Charity

Review the challenge from conference 5: Put humility into action this week by honestly putting yourself in the last place in some way.

Questions for meditation and discussion

1. "Love Him, first of all, with an immense love; then read in His eyes and in His heart what you must be for others who, after all, are not really 'others' since they are, like you, members of His Mystical Body, or at least called to be such." (page 141)

   What must we be for others? Be specific. Identify who some of the "others" are and what we can be for each of them.

2. "We are, without intending it, excellent instruments of humiliation and mortification for each other. Love others, not in spite of that, but because of it." (page 143)

   Think of something that has happened to you that caused you humiliation. How did you react? How could you have reacted with love and gratitude?

3. "We have a tendency to become obsessed by the faults of those around us. That is understandable: it is their faults which make us suffer, and this suffering, in turn, reminds us of them continually. Yet do not I, myself, have even worse faults? We always come back to the case of the mote and the beam! Faults are ugly. Why not look at the virtues which are beautiful? I told you that you must apply yourselves to seeing things with the eyes of Jesus, as He sees them, to loving what He loves....

   "Do not judge intentions.... As much as you can, ascribe good intentions to your neighbor." (pages 144–145)

Have you ever ascribed bad intentions to someone only to find out later the story behind the story? Have you ever imagined the tone of an e-mail rather than taking the message at face value? Has anyone misread your intentions? How does this resonate with you? What does this teach us about empathy?

4. "We must forget ourselves. A person who forgets himself brings joy to those around him. He quickens hearts everywhere he goes. Goodness attracts goodness—and what is more, it gives birth to goodness. It radiates something already heavenly. On the other hand, spitefulness causes sadness, closes hearts, hardens faces, and brings a cold chill wherever it appears.... The spiteful person starts putting facts together which in reality are totally unrelated, in order to make his neighbor's offenses seem greater, to put his neighbor in an inexcusable position in order to excuse himself. The Devil fans these smoldering embers." (pages 148–149)

   When have you allowed the Devil to fan the smoldering embers? What was the result? How could you have acted in a way that radiates goodness?

5. "There is a very beautiful thought to consider here. It is that you can say to Him, 'Jesus, to love my neighbor as You love me is impossible with my poor heart so small, so narrow, so mean. Therefore, in giving me this precept, You must give me Your own Heart, to fulfill it.' How could He resist such logic—logic that must make Him smile?" (page 157)

   Prepare a prayer for the times when it is difficult to love your neighbor as yourself.

6. "Have you meditated on the Last Judgment, which will be based entirely on the virtue of charity?

   "'For I was hungry, and you gave me to eat; I was thirsty and you gave me to drink; I was a stranger and you took me in; naked, and you covered me; sick, and you visited me; I was in prison, and you came to me.... As long as you did it to one of these my least brethren, you did it to me.... Come, you blessed of my Father.'" (pages 158–159)

Think of your role in the community:

I was a child and you provided for me.

I was a caregiver and you looked out for my well-being.

I was new to the neighborhood (or parish or office or school), and you introduced yourself to me.

I was a volunteer and you thanked me.

I was a parent and you encouraged me.

I was a spouse and you listened to me.

Now list some more roles that reflect opportunities for charity in your community.

This week's challenge

Live out one of the roles you listed in question 6.

Conference 7

The Apostolate

Review the challenge from conference 6: Live out one of the roles you wrote in question 6 from the last conference.

Questions for meditation and discussion

1. "You know well that it is the task of the whole Church to continue to develop the mission of salvation of all whom Christ entrusts to her. This task belongs not only to the hierarchy, but to the laity also, by virtue of their membership in the Mystical Body of Christ, and of their participation in His mission and His royal priesthood. They have the right, the duty, and the honor—confirmed and affirmed by the sacraments of Baptism and Confirmation—to exercise the apostolate of the Church in the way which is proper to them." (page 164)

   How do you think you are exercising or can "exercise the apostolate of the Church in the way which is proper" to you?

2. "But you know, before the apostolate of word and action, there is the apostolate of prayer and suffering, without which the external apostolate would be nothing—nothing at all. Words and actions come only in last place, after what I call the apostolate of silence in love, which was the great apostolate of Jesus and Mary at Nazareth for thirty years." (page 167)

   How can you use prayer and suffering to be an apostle for the Church?

3. "What is the center and source of life of the Church? The Host in the tabernacle, the little, the silent Host, the praying Host, the loving Host.... Be a praying and loving host,

and you will send forth rays like the Host, and God will give you all those who 'voyage' with you, your neighbors, all those whom you love and whose salvation you ardently desire." (page 174)

The Host is Jesus in the appearance of bread. It is described as little, silent, praying, and loving. We can be more like Christ in those ways. Can you think of a time or a situation when being "little" make you more like Christ? Being silent? Prayerful? Loving? Try to be specific, using real or possible scenarios that you might find yourself in.

4. Have you ever spent time in adoration of the Blessed Sacrament?

5. "You know that the prayer of prayers is the Mass; perfect adoration, perfect expiation, perfect thanksgiving, it is also perfect supplication of the immolated Jesus; it is the dearest treasure of the apostolate." (page 180)

   How is the Mass a "treasure" for you?

6. "He Himself needs others, because He wishes to use them as His instruments.... So many diverse fields of activity are open today to those who want to be apostles." (page 187)

   How are you currently being used as an instrument for Christ in the community? Do you desire to be used more? In what way? (Do you have gifts you feel called to share but have not yet found the way to do it?)

7. "Do not be afraid to pronounce and to repeat often the name of *Jesus*. It is not a matter of indifference whether you always say, 'the Lord,' 'Christ,' or 'Jesus.' There is a very special grace attached to the name of *Jesus*. The evangelists use the name *Jesus*, and St. John calls Mary *Mater Jesu*: 'Mother of Jesus.' Remember that it is His Father who gave Him this name and who revealed it to Mary by the angel Gabriel." (pages 190–191)

   Try repeating the name of Jesus when you are in need of peace or when facing temptation. Did you feel differently afterward?

8. "Remember that each soul won wins others, and that you will be forever the spiritual father or mother of a multitude of elect who will come to seek you out upon your arrival at the door of Paradise, or whom you will receive when they arrive." (pages 191–192)

   Meditate on this beautiful scene. Who are some who came before you who were spiritual mothers and fathers to you? How will you greet them? Who do you think will seek you out as a spiritual mother or father?

This week's challenge

Find a new way to be an instrument for Christ.

Conference 8

The Cross

Review the challenge from conference 7: Find a new way to be an instrument for Christ.

Questions for meditation and discussion

1. "The Cross is a marvelous invention of divine mercy which gives us the occasion to prove to Jesus that we love Him. What is a love that does not prove itself? I told you love is a choice. What merit is there in choosing Jesus if we only have to follow him on a path of roses?" (page 196)

    When you suffer, as we all do, how do you usually react?

2. "A great cross is, very often, the prelude to a great grace, even for an unbeliever. Suffering ripens the soul, sometimes very quickly. A great trial can, with one stroke, detach a soul from all that is created; it can be the source of total conversion." (page 199)

   Have you experienced a conversion as a result of a great trial, or have you seen this happen to someone close to you?

3. "Suffering is an expiation of sin. Jesus willed to wash our crimes in His Blood, but, in order to participate in this sorrowful Redemption, we must know also how to be, at least in part, 'a man of sorrows.' It is an inescapable law; we must pass that way." (page 200)

   Prepare a prayer of thanksgiving for suffering.

4. "Suffering is a goldmine to exploit for saving souls, for helping missionaries, for being a hidden apostle. What happiness it is to be able to suffer when we cannot act!" (page 203)

   Do you have a focus for your sufferings, so that when they come your way, you are prepared to offer them up for that intention?

5. "In our days, how many plans we make, little calculations—very often unconscious, I must say—which are made simply to avoid suffering!" (page 204)

Parents want to protect their children. Are we doing a disservice to children—whether our own children, our grandchildren, or other children in our lives—by not allowing them to suffer? How can we teach them to suffer gracefully?

6. "Another great treasure of suffering is that it teaches us to be compassionate. When one has suffered himself, he understands much better the sufferings of others." (page 212)

   Have you been the beneficiary of comfort from someone who has suffered in the same way that you have? How did the comfort given by that person differ from the comfort given by those who have not experienced the same sort of pain?

This week's challenge

> "Have a very great devotion to that extraordinary sign which has become ordinary through routine—the Sign of the Cross. If, each time you make it, you will it and believe it, you bring upon yourself the infinite goodness of the Father of Mercies; the Spirit of love grows in your hearts, and you put on Jesus Christ again. You cover yourself instantly with His Blood, which liberates and purifies you. You make the Redemption yours. You unite yourself to the Lamb slain and raised to life, who is always living to make intercession for you in Heaven. You glorify the Holy Trinity. One gesture—it takes you a few seconds; you can make it a hundred times a day, and it plunges you each time into eternity. There is even a certain physical satisfaction in covering yourself with the Sign of the Cross." (page 214)

Each day this week, make a conscious effort when you make the Sign of the Cross to be attentive to all that it means.

Conference 9

The Eucharist

Review the challenge from conference 8: Each day this week, make a conscious effort to be aware of making the Sign of the Cross and all that it means.

Questions for meditation and discussion

1. "The Mass is the divine act around which the life of the Church gravitates and of which she is the radiance; the center from which she receives all impulses and toward which she is continually directed; the living source from which she proceeds and the ocean to which she returns." (page 221)

   The Mass is so important, yet most of us attend only once a week. What keeps us from making the Mass a higher priority?

2. "The faithful, in virtue of their royal priesthood, join in the offering of the Eucharist. They likewise exercise that priesthood in receiving sacraments, in prayer and thanksgiving, in the witness of a holy life, and by self-denial and active charity." (page 227)

   Being part of the royal priesthood means that we are to bring holiness to every aspect of our life and every activity in our day. In what ways do you bring holiness into your daily life? In what other ways can we do this?

3. "He did will to die, but He did not want to leave. He did not want to go away from us and leave us alone.... [So] He instituted the Holy Eucharist." (page 239)

   Since Jesus is truly present in the Eucharist and we truly consume His Body and Blood at Communion, we carry Him with us as we leave Mass. Are you conscious of this? How does it change your behavior?

4. "These words, 'Behold the Lamb of God, who takes away the sins,' and 'I am not worthy, but speak only a word,' are the most beautiful, the most complete, and the most marvelous preparation for Communion." (page 243)

    The Church, in her love for us, has given us the words to prepare ourselves for Communion. But we must say them and believe them. To be a disciple takes discipline. What can we do to be better prepared to receive Christ in the Eucharist?

5. "At the moment of receiving Communion, say to Jesus, 'Jesus, I come to You because I am weak, because I am

miserable, because I am a sinner. I come to You because I have so much need of You." (page 244)

Do you feel a great need to receive Communion?

6. Have you dedicated your family and home to the Sacred Heart of Jesus?

This week's challenge

"Be an apostle of holy Mass and Communion. Do everything possible to facilitate daily communion.... Urge souls to come!" (page 245)

This week, make an effort to go to Mass at least one more time than is usual for you. And bring someone with you!

Conference 10

Jesus, Mary, and the Saints

Review the challenge from conference 9: This week, make an effort to go to Mass at least one more time than is usual for you. And bring someone with you!

Questions for meditation and discussion

1. "In our time Jesus also wants hidden saints like the 'woman of Nazareth,' who distinguish themselves in nothing exteriorly, but who burn interiorly." (page 259)

   What can you do to imitate Mary's simplicity?

2. "At the origin of the redemption of those souls whom God has resolved to save through you must be also your loving abandonment, your *Ecce ancilla* ('Behold the handmaid'), your *fiat*." (page 260).

   What can you do to imitate Mary's abandonment?

3. "She knew that all these crosses were, in the divine plan, necessary for the salvation of men and the greatest proof of love which Jesus could give her." (page 262)

   What can you do to imitate Mary's heroism of the cross?

4. "In her *fiat* at Nazareth there is something of the impulse of a mother who wants to prevent her child from falling into

the flames, for she realized more than anyone else what sin is, what Hell is. So she cried, 'Yes, let me receive the sword, the piercing lance at Golgotha. I consent to see Jesus suffer and die to save my other children.'" (page 262)

What can you do to imitate Mary's thirst for souls?

____

____

____

____

____

5. "The absence of sin is a condition; but what we need beyond that is the positive beauty of sanctifying grace—that is to say, the Holy Trinity in us. That is purity: Mary, full of grace." (page 264)

   How can we imitate Mary's pure love?

____

____

____

____

____

6. "He [Peter] needed a lesson. So he got one.... He received grace, he received mercy, he repented, he wept, and he was

more filled with grace afterward than if he had not denied Christ." (pages 269–270)

Have you ever failed and become stronger and wiser for it?

7. "In the current of your daily life, in the course of your days, you must also say, 'It is the Lord.' Whether a contradiction or a thorn comes: 'It is the Lord!' Whether a joy or a pleasure: 'It is He; I recognize Him everywhere! I see nothing anymore but Him: *Dominus est!* Jesus, You may hide Yourself behind secondary causes, behind creatures: You will not fool me. I shall always recognize You.'" (page 271)

   Do you recognize the Lord in your daily life in both the joys and the difficulties?

8. Regarding the entire St. Thérèse study, what conference or aspect of this program was most beneficial to you on your personal spiritual journey?

Challenge going forth

Share this with others! Consider leading a group!

An Invitation

Reader, the book that you hold in your hands was published by Sophia Institute Press. Sophia Institute seeks to nurture the spiritual, moral, and cultural life of souls and to spread the Gospel of Christ in conformity with the authentic teachings of the Roman Catholic Church.

Our press fulfills this mission by offering translations, reprints, and new publications that afford readers a rich source of the enduring wisdom of mankind.

We also operate two popular online Catholic resources: CrisisMagazine.com and CatholicExchange.com.

Crisis Magazine provides insightful cultural analysis that arms readers with the arguments necessary for navigating the ideological and theological minefields of the day. *Catholic Exchange* provides world news from a Catholic perspective as well as daily devotionals and articles that will help you to grow in holiness and live a life consistent with the teachings of the Church.

Sophia Institute Press also serves as the publisher for the Thomas More College of Liberal Arts and Holy Spirit College. Both colleges provide university-level education under the guiding light of Catholic teaching. If you know a young person seeking a college that takes seriously the adventure of learning and the quest for truth, please bring these institutions to his attention.

www.SophiaInstitute.com
www.CatholicExchange.com
www.CrisisMagazine.com

Sophia Institute Press® is a registered trademark of Sophia Institute.
Sophia Institute is a tax-exempt institution as defined by the Internal Revenue Code, Section 501(c)(3). Tax I.D. 22-2548708.